BRITAIN IN OLD PHOTOGRAPHS

MARGATE

A SECOND SELECTION

RICHARD CLEMENTS

SUTTON PUBLISHING LIMITED

Sutton Publishing Limited
Phoenix Mill · Thrupp · Stroud
Gloucestershire · GL5 2BU

First published 1997

Reprinted in 2002

Copyright © Richard Clements, 1997

Cover photographs: *front*: coach and horses
outside the Cliftonville Hotel, Ethelbert
Crescent, 2 Septebmer 1911; *back*: suffragettes
outside the Theatre Royal in Prince's Street,
c. 1912.

British Library Cataloguing in Publication Data
A catalogue record for this book is available from the
British Library.

ISBN 0-7509-1399-1

Typeset in 10/12 Perpetua.
Typesetting and origination by
Sutton Publishing Limited.
Printed in Great Britain by
J. H. Haynes & Co. Ltd, Sparkford.

The Parade, a busy scene, *c.* 1905.

CONTENTS

The crew of His Majesty's Coastguard at Margate, 1907. In the centre is George William Baker, the chief officer.

INTRODUCTION

This second selection of photographs of old Margate has again been taken from my own collection of stereographs and postcards. The nineteenth-century illustrations are mainly stereographs, while those from the twentieth century are postcards.

The origins of the town can be traced back to about 1050 when a fishing village developed, later known as 'Meregate', meaning a gate or way to the sea. By the end of the thirteenth century this name had become 'Margate'. During the first quarter of the nineteenth century, Margate began to develop as a holiday resort with the early steam boats making the journey from London in six hours. With the arrival of the South Eastern Railway via Ramsgate in 1846, London became even closer, and by 1863 the London, Chatham & Dover Railway arrived on the direct route of 74 miles via Faversham, making the town accessible to London in two hours.

Included in this book, together with the town areas of Margate and Cliftonville, are the villages of Garlinge, Northdown, Reading Street and Kingsgate. At the beginning of the twentieth century they were villages, but over the years Garlinge and Northdown have been swallowed up by Margate and Cliftonville, while Reading Street and Kingsgate have become part of Broadstairs.

No attempt is made within this book to tell the history of the town, but instead the main aim has been to illustrate for the reader as many aspects of Victorian and Edwardian life in Margate as possible. The reader will see how the area had developed since the middle of the nineteenth century, or, in some areas, how very little has changed.

Much of my research into this book has involved visiting the scene of the illustration and making a comparison with what exists there today. I would suggest the reader makes the same comparison as I have found this to be one of the most enjoyable aspects of the project.

Richard Clements, 1997

The Hope & Anchor public house, 173–5 High Street, when the proprietor was Jack Crowson, 1909. This building was demolished in 1953 to make way for the flats that now occupy this part of Margate High Street.

THE TOWN

The Parade seen in a postcard published by Goodmans Studio of 57 Fort Road, Margate, c. 1910. On the left are the Royal York Mansions, the entrance to Duke Street, and the Parade post office owned by Miss Beatrice Hellis. Evans the chemist at 1 High Street remained as such until the 1980s.

Canterbury Road at its junction with Rancorn Road, *c.* 1924. Most of the buildings still exist, except that the two lodging houses on the left, nos 56 and 58, had been demolished by 1929. The houses on the right, nos 123–9, have now been converted to shop premises.

Hatfeild Road viewed from Sea View Terrace, *c.* 1905. At this time almost every house here is listed in the directory as a 'lodging house'.

The Royal Sea Bathing Hospital was believed to have been the oldest orthopaedic hospital in the world, and was founded by Dr John Coakley Lettsom on 2 July 1791. It is seen here in about 1905. The four stone pillars and pediment were originally the façade of Lord Holland's mansion, Holland House, at Kingsgate; how they were transported to the hospital site is unknown.

An 'outside ward' at the Royal Sea Bathing Hospital, c. 1920. The hospital pioneered open-air treatment for patients suffering from tubercular complaints, as seen here. In the left background can be seen the chemist shop owned by G.P. Harkness at 97 Canterbury Road.

The surfboat disaster memorial was erected in October 1899 in memory of the nine men who lost their lives when the surfboat *Friend to all Nations* was lost on the morning of 2 December 1897.

Buenos Ayres Road and the approach to Margate West railway station, 1920.

Eaton Road, 1913. The row of houses on the left, named Belgrave Villas, were erected in 1865 by Thomas Reeve, who at that time was the Margate Borough Surveyor and Sanitary Inspector. The brooks opposite were drained shortly after this time and the area was later developed into what is now Dreamland Amusement Park. Construction of the houses on the right, and the remainder of Eaton Road, commenced in 1867.

Vicarage Place looking towards Ramsgate Road, c. 1912. In the background is 4 Ramsgate Road.

Helena Avenue viewed from the junction with Alexandra Road, and looking towards Ramsgate Road, *c.* 1910. Many of the houses are listed in the directory as 'lodging houses', indicating the vast influx of visitors to Margate during the Edwardian period. Note the milk delivery cart in the foreground together with the milkman who kindly posed for the photographer.

Beatrice Road viewed from the junction with Ramsgate Road, 1907. The two houses on the left are known as Denmark Villas at 57 and 55 Beatrice Road, while on the right is the entrance to Helena Avenue.

Ramsgate Road viewed from the entrance to Connaught Road, 1907. The houses from right to left, are nos 3 to 15. In the background is the bank and bridge carrying the London, Chatham & Dover Railway line from Margate West railway station to Broadstairs and Ramsgate.

Buckingham Road viewed from the junction with Tivoli Road, looking towards Ramsgate Road, 1907. The building at the end of the road on the right is the back of 13 and 15 Ramsgate Road, seen in the top photograph.

Marine Terrace looking east from the Cinque Ports public house, *c.* 1875. The Cinque Ports first appears in the directories as an 'inn' in about 1820.

Marine Terrace was built as the 'New Road' in 1809, and the buildings that now form Marine Terrace were completed by 1835 as 'gentlemen's residences', with the Cinque Ports public house at the western end, and the Kent public house at the eastern end. Here Marine Terrace is viewed westward from the Kent public house in about 1875.

Albert Terrace viewed from Marine Terrace, *c.* 1875.

Albert Terrace viewed from Marine Terrace, *c.* 1905. Marine Drive, on the left, was constructed in 1878 to join Marine Terrace to the Parade and harbour areas; until this time access between the two had been via Upper Marine Terrace, on the right of the picture, and the High Street. The clock tower was constructed in 1889, and the tram system arrived in 1901. The large building on the right of Albert Terrace now houses the Stanley Casino.

Marine Terrace, as it was originally built, *c.* 1875. Some of Marine Terrace was constructed by Harold Woodward, who, during the same period, was responsible for the construction of Fort Paragon and much of Zion Place. By 1930 all of these houses had been converted into shop premises.

Marine Terrace, a similar view to that on page 14, but taken in about 1905, with a 'Hovis' baker's delivery cart in the foreground.

Marine Terrace, c. 1905. By this time many of the houses had already been converted to shop premises. An early car is seen parked outside 30 Marine Terrace, now Top Fayre, a gift shop typical of the seafront in the 1990s.

The West End Hotel and Restaurant owned by Gordon Fowler at 49, 50 and 51 Marine Terrace, where 'beanfeasts and banquets' are advertised, 1927. On the left is the confectioners owned by Douglas Batchelor, and on the right, the Cinque Ports Hotel.

Albert Terrace viewed from Marine Terrace, *c.* 1870. The tall house with the flag is Bramfield House, built in 1840, and the home from 1861 of Frederick Hodges, founder of the first organized fire brigade in Margate. Albert Terrace was known as Hazardous Row until 1832, and as Lansells Place until 1868. The buildings on the left are the backs of those in the High Street, before the building of Marine Drive.

Another view of Albert Terrace and Marine Drive, *c.* 1925. Tram no. 3 is seen departing from the clock tower to travel towards the harbour. The clock tower was erected to commemorate the Golden Jubilee of Queen Victoria in 1887, and was handed over to the Corporation on 24 May 1889.

Longhi and Sons Restaurant at 22, 23 and 24 Marine Drive, 1928. On the left is the photographer's shop owned by Charles Davis, and in the background are houses in Albert Terrace.

The Parade, c. 1912. The White Hart Hotel was built in 1876 on the site of the earlier White Hart, seen on page 96. The building was one of the premier hotels in the town and survived until April 1967. On the right are the Royal York Mansions and the shop premises of William Woodgate, tobacconist, and Albert Norman Reeves, confectioner. On the left is the Royal Albion Hotel.

The Parade, looking towards the High Street between 1876, when the White Hart Hotel was constructed, and 1880. Note that the Imperial Hotel has yet to be built at the lower end of the High Street.

The Parade looking in the opposite direction, c. 1910. On the left is the Droit House, and in the centre the Ship Hotel and Metropole Hotel, both demolished as part of the Fort Road improvement scheme between December 1937 and April 1939. Centre right is the original Fort Hill.

Post Office Margate. Opened by the Rt. Hon. Herbert Samuel, postmaster General July 19th 1[...]

Opening of the post office in Cecil Square by the Postmaster General, the Right Hon. Herbert Samuel MP, accompanied by the mayor, Alderman William H. White, 19 July 1910. The press report in the local newspaper informs us that 'a great crowd assembled in Cecil Square, and when the Postmaster General had declared the post office open, there was an immediate rush of customers to the various departments to purchase stamps, post a letter, and send a telegram. There is a spacious telegraph room on the first floor, and upon the second floor, a commodious room for future telephone purposes. At the back of the building is a sorting office with separate accommodation for the convenience of naval postman from HM ships lying off Margate. The premises are heated by hot water radiators and lighted throughout by electricity.'

High Street, the lower part, looking towards the Parade before the building of the Imperial Hotel, *c.* 1875. The building on the right with the first floor veranda is now 23 and 25 High Street, the same facia and the veranda being retained to this day.

The post office, grocers and general stores at 30 Victoria Road when the postmaster was H. Bailey, 1912. The bicycle costs £4 10*s* and is described as 'the cheapest bicycle eyes have ever seen'.

Wright's family butchers shop at 105 High Street, *c.* 1913. It was owned by Everard Wright, who was in business at these premises from 1913 to 1919. At the end of the nineteenth century the premises were known as Peterkin's, music sellers, and by 1900 had become Pilcher's fruit store. William Dray continued the fruit business before the premises were taken over by Kemp's watchmakers in 1905. George Kemp remained in business until Everard Wright opened in 1913. By 1920, Benjamin Parker had taken over the premises as a fishmongers, and the shop remained with the family until the mid-1960s.

Hawley Square, *c*. 1908. The square was developed in 1770 and nos 30 to 37 on the south side of the square are seen here.

Shaftesbury House in Upper Marine Terrace, viewed from Albert Terrace, *c*. 1912. This part of Marine Terrace was renamed Marine Gardens in the mid-1930s, but is known locally as Elephant Hill after the Elephant public house that stood at the junction of High Street and Marine Gardens until 1972. Shaftesbury House was purchased in 1882 by Mr G. Williams, a wealthy Londoner, who presented it to the YMCA in 1887 for use as a seaside home for poor children from the East End. It was named after the Victorian reformer Lord Shaftesbury, and later became a temperance hotel. It was destroyed by fire in 1988.

The staff of Worlds Stores Limited pose for the photographer outside their store at 90 High Street, *c.* 1920.

The Pumper windmill, *c.* 1910. It was built at Drapers between 1858 and 1872 and was used for pumping water. By the time this photograph was taken it had fallen into disrepair, the cap and sweeps having been destroyed in 1894. The house on the right was owned by Miss Hester and was known as Watermill Cottage. It is now 177 College Road.

Drapers Mill, one of three windmills that once stood on this site. The remaining mill, a smock mill built in about 1845 by John Holman of Canterbury, and seen here, is now fully restored.

Dane Park was opened by the Lord Mayor of London on 1 June 1898. The area was previously farmland and was purchased at auction in 1895 by a local resident, John Woodward, and presented by him to the Borough of Margate as a park of 25 acres. In the background is the Royal School for the Deaf, built in 1875.

The greengrocers shop at 1 Dane Road, owned by Ernest A. French, *c.* 1910. The road on the left is Dane Hill. These premises are now used as a café, and are opposite the old gas works.

Bath Road, looking towards Northumberland Road (later renamed Northdown Road), 1907. The houses seen here are 1 to 9 Carn Brea.

Milton Square viewed from Milton Road, *c.* 1910. The grocery shop on the corner of Shakespeare Road was owned by Rowland Beerling, and numbered 15 Milton Square.

The town hall and market-place, *c.* 1904. The town hall consists of three buildings, that part to the right dating from 1820, the main part in the centre of the photograph from 1898. The earlier part of the building housed the police station until the present building was opened on Fort Hill in the late 1950s. The old police station now houses the Margate Museum. The building to the left is the Bulls Head public house, built in 1880.

The Queens Highcliffe Hotel dates from the early years of the twentieth century, and was taken over by the Butlins organization in 1955. Following two serious fires, the building was demolished in 1974. A 1920s carnival is seen passing in the foreground. Queen's Court now stands on this site.

Fort Crescent, constructed between 1825 and 1829. This view, taken in about 1875, shows that little of the structure has altered in over 120 years.

The Paragon, c. 1875. It was built in 1830 by Harold Woodward, a local builder, and father of John Woodward who gave Dane Park to the town. In the background, part of Fort Crescent can be seen at its junction with Zion Place.

Ethelbert Crescent viewed from Ethelbert Terrace, 1920. On the right is the junction with Athelstan Road and on page 73 a tram is seen negotiating this tight turn. In the centre is the Cliftonville Hotel, built in 1868 and demolished in 1962.

Fort Crescent and the Fort bandstand, c. 1906. The Winter Gardens now stand on this site. Tram 32 can be seen making its way towards Fort Hill before descending to the Parade and harbour.

Zion Place viewed from the junction with Cliff Terrace, *c.* 1925. The block of three houses on the right was known as Trafalgar Place, and the small road on the right was Pleasant Place. This area had been developed by 1850. All the buildings on the west side were demolished between November 1961 and May 1962 during the council's compulsory purchase scheme, as were those on the east side in the centre of the picture.

Zion Place, again looking towards what is now Northdown Road, *c.* 1908. All the buildings on the right of the photograph, the Randolph Hotel and nos 14 to 28, disappeared in 1962, and the road to its junction with Northdown Road was straightened.

Ethelbert Road viewed from the junction with Cliff Terrace, *c.* 1875. Development of the road commenced in 1857, and these buildings were constructed in the early 1860s. The council took over the road in 1865, at which time it was the eastern boundary of the borough.

Ethelbert Road, viewed from the junction with Northumberland Road (now Northdown Road), 1913. The two ladies are standing outside no. 60. In March 1914 building started on the Rehoboth Strict Baptist chapel on the piece of waste ground to the left.

Parr's Bank Limited at 10 Cliftonville Parade, Alexandra Road, Cliftonville, when the manager was Ernest Kingston, 1911. Shortly after the First World War, the road numbering was altered, and the premises became the National Provincial & Union Bank of England Limited at 85 Northdown Road. The building is at the junction with Dalby Road.

Alexandra Road (later renamed Northdown Road), *c.* 1905. On the left is Cliftonville Parade built in 1880, and includes the boot-makers shop of Joseph Jones. Behind this shop is Parr's Bank seen in the top photograph. St Stephen's Wesleyan Chapel was built between 1876 and 1878, and the tower was erected in 1886. The houses on the right are now shops at 88 and 90 Northdown Road. At this time the row of houses on the right between Wilderness Hill and Clifton Gardens were known as Clifton Terrace.

Northumberland Road, Cliftonville, 1906. The photograph shows the houses and shops on the south side of what is now Northdown Road, between the junctions of Bath Road and Dane Hill.

The tailors shop of Arthur E. Villette situated at 33 Northumberland Road, on the corner with Ethelbert Road. These premises were later renumbered as 49 Northdown Road. This photograph was taken in 1913 soon after the shop opened for business.

Northdown Road at the junction with Godwin Road, *c.* 1910. At this time the row of shops between Sweyn Road and Godwin Road was known as The Broadway.

Northdown Road, viewed from the junction with Clarendon Road, *c.* 1910. In the centre background can be seen the tower of St Paul's Church. The buildings to the right of the tram are Magdala Villas, built in 1860, were the first to be constructed in Northdown Road. The shop on the left is Rhodes Outfitters at nos 54 and 56 (now Dillons post office) and next door at no. 52 is William Petts ironmongers (now Boots Chemist).

The International Tea Company Stores Limited at 5 Cliftonville Parade, Alexandra Road, where the staff pose outside their shop in 1906. In about 1920 the premises were renumbered as 75 Northdown Road.

Northdown Road, viewed from the corner of Lyndhurst Avenue, *c.* 1930. The shop on the extreme right is that of Maison Tessier hairdressers at no. 235, and at no. 233 is the Floral Hall flower shop. Next to them are the premises of Munro Cobb furnishers.

Montrose Ladies College in Lower Northdown Road, 1905. The buildings are now part of Laleham School. In the foreground is the entrance to the private road that carried the tramway from what is now Northdown Park Road to Northdown Road. The private road remains to this day as a footpath.

L.B. King & Company were wine, spirit and beer merchants with shop premises at 43 Northumberland Road, Cliftonville. The photograph, taken in about 1914, shows the delivery service operated by the company. Road renumbering took place in about 1920, and roads previously known as Northumberland Road and Alexandra Road became part of Northdown Road. King's then became 59 Northdown Road. Rigden & Co. were brewers, with a local store in Mill Lane, Margate and head offices at The Brewery, Court Street, Faversham.

The Parade, a panorama photographed from the pier, 1907. From the left the buildings are the White Hart Hotel and the Royal York Hotel at the junction of Duke Street. Across the junction at nos 12 and 13 is George's Restaurant owned by George Downs, at no. 14 the Chamber of Commerce Information Bureau, and at 14a, Paramores, railway and forwarding agents. Thynne's drapers is at no. 15, and at no. 16 Miss Mitchell's Repository and Servants Registry. The last building in this block is the London City and Midland Bank Limited. Then the junction with Market Street is reached, and the first of the buildings facing the camera at no. 19 is the Avondale Restaurant owned by Joseph Reynolds. Beaumont & Son, hatters, is at no. 20 and Edward Lawrence, a tobacconist at no. 21. Tannenbaum Brothers, a jewellers, is at no. 22. The Parade finished at this point with Evans the Chemist at 1 High Street. Having clearly identified each of these commercial premises the reader will find it possible to compare this view with the shops and buildings that exist there today.

HARBOUR,
JETTY & BEACH

Holiday-makers enjoying the water at Margate, c. 1910. The picture is by local beach photographer,
W.P. Dobbs of 16 Clifton Gardens.

The Droit House at the entrance to the pier, *c.* 1875. Constructed in 1829, the building was used by the Pier and Harbour Company, and it was here that the various pier dues were collected. In front stand the horse-drawn cabs, awaiting the more affluent passengers from the London boats.

The Droit House, pier and jetty, *c.* 1920. The London boat can be seen arriving at the jetty, while the horse-drawn cabs still wait on the pier. German bombs destroyed the Droit House in October 1940 and January 1941, but it was rebuilt to the original design in 1947.

The hoy barge being unloaded on the pier, *c.* 1905. The crane can be seen unloading barrels for Crawford & Company Limited, wine and spirit merchants, which had premises at 5 and 6 The Parade and a store in Mansion Street.

The harbour, September 1904. The canoe *Tilikum* arrived at Margate on 2 September 1904 having completed a 40,000-mile journey starting in Victoria, British Columbia, from where she left on 21 May 1901. The journey took her captain, John C. Voss, to Fiji, Australia, New Zealand, South Africa and St Helena, before arriving in England. In the background is the Royal York Hotel in The Parade, with Dunn's Parade Restaurant at the junction of Duke Street.

The sea front, as seen on a postcard that was one of a series produced in 1907. Bathing machines can be seen on the sands, while a tram makes its way to the terminus at Westbrook. The church in the background is Holy Trinity, destroyed by bombing in 1943.

Children enjoying a donkey ride on the sands, August 1913. The beach photographer responsible for this photograph came from the Clock Tower Studio at 1 Marine Terrace. The Margate donkeyman at this time was Archie Brown who kept thirty donkeys on the sands opposite Marine Terrace.

Margate sands viewed from the jetty, *c*. 1924. Marine Drive, connecting the harbour area to Marine Terrace, is seen in the centre of the photograph. The Imperial Hotel, recently restored to its original splendour, was built in 1880.

The Marine Sands viewed from the opposite direction to that seen above, *c*. 1908. In the centre background is Marine Drive, and to the right, Albert Terrace.

Holiday-makers pose on a bathing cart, *c*. 1910. This was another photograph from the Clock Tower Studio at 1 Marine Terrace.

A group of bathers pose for the photographer, *c*. 1924. This picture was taken by Sunbeam Photo Limited, who at that time operated from workshops at 45 Dane Hill.

Bathing machines lined up at Walpole Bay, 21 September 1913.

A group pose for the camera on Marine Sands, *c.* 1910. On the right is the Cinque Ports public house.

Marine Terrace, *c.* 1875. The bridge in the foreground carried pedestrians over a pathway along which the bathing machines, horses and donkeys were taken to the beach from their stables. It was demolished in 1878 when Marine Drive was built.

The beach at high tide, *c.* 1875. The bathing machines are pulled up to the high water mark and Albert Terrace is seen in the background.

Walpole Bay, 21 September 1913, when the horses and bathing-machine attendants pose for the photographer with the bathing station in the background.

Pettman's Sea Bathing Pavilion between Newgate Gap and Walpole Bay, c. 1910. This view is looking towards Newgate Gap, while the top photograph shows the Walpole Bay end of the pavilion.

Concert parties performing on the sands were an important part of entertainment life at Margate and other resorts until the summer of 1939. Harry Gold, born Patrick Henry James Ricks in Jersey in 1866, was one of the most famous, and formed several troupes that performed on Margate sands. He died in 1946.

Gold's Dandy Coons seen on a souvenir postcard produced in 1907. Other concert parties which performed at Margate were billed as Gold's Smart Serenaders, Gold's Margate Pierrots, and Gold's Margate Yachtsmen.

Gold's Margate Pierrots on the Marine Sands during the summer of 1904.

Harry Gold's Entertainers on the Marine Sands, *c.* 1930.

Bathers, bathing-cart crew and horses pose for a photograph, *c.* 1910. Beach photographers were plentiful during this period, and holiday pictures such as this one were printed as postcards and were on the way to family and friends later the same day. In 1910 the last postal collection in Margate was 9.45 p.m. (9.20 p.m. on Sundays), for delivery by 8.15 a.m. the following morning in London.

Marine Sands, a beach scene showing the bathing carts, *c.* 1875.

Marine Sands, a crowded scene, *c.* 1905. The bathing machines are lined up against a background which has changed little to this day. The beach clothing is interesting on what appears to be a warm summer's day!

Bathers waiting to be taken by the bathing cart to the bathing machines on the Marine Sands, *c*. 1906.

The entrance to the jetty, *c*. 1908. In the background on the pier can be seen the boathouse for the lifeboat, seen in more detail on page 57. The building to the right of the photograph, on the jetty, was known as a 'camera obscura'. Through a rotating lens in the roof of the building, a photographic image of the surrounding view was reflected on to a large white dish within the building for the public to view.

Margate jetty, viewed from the end of the jetty, *c.* 1870. Building commenced in 1853 following demolition of the original wooden jetty built by Dr Daniel Jarvis in 1824. The wrought-iron structure was 1,500 feet long, and was the first to have screw piles, invented by the pier engineer, Eugenius Birch. The jetty was opened to the public in April 1855.

Another view of the jetty before the addition of the extension in 1875, *c.* 1870.

The jetty extension was built in 1875, the hexagonal shape allowing three vessels to berth at one time. There was also a central pavilion, seen here in this 1914 postcard, together with a bandstand.

This aerial view of the jetty extension clearly shows the hexagonal shape. There were three tiers of landing stages, thus allowing use of the jetty whatever the state of the tide. On the left of the photograph is the paddlesteamer *Royal Eagle* which, at 1,539 tons, was one of the largest of the regular visitors. Owned by the General Steam Navigation Company, she was built at Birkenhead in 1932, and saw service until 1953. On the right is the *Queen of Thanet*, owned by the New Medway Steam Packet Company. Built at Glasgow in 1916, at 792 tons, she remained in service until 1951.

Lifeboat *Quiver No. 1* outside the lifeboat station on the pier soon after arriving in 1866. The location of the lifeboat station at this time can be seen more clearly on page 54. The boat was a gift to the National Lifeboat Institution by the Quiver Lifeboat Fund, and was 34 feet long with 12 oars. Built by Messrs Forrest and Sons of Limehouse, London, she could carry forty persons in addition to the crew. The boat remained at Margate until 1883, and during this time was launched thirty-eight times, rescuing seventy people in all.

The surfboat memorial in Margate Cemetery. On 2 December 1897, the surfboat *Friend to all Nations* was launched in a storm to go to the aid of a vessel, the *Persian Empire*. Soon after launching the surfboat capsized, and eight crew, together with Charles Troughton, Superintendent of the Margate Ambulance Corps, lost their lives. The memorial is inscribed: 'In memory of nine heroic men who lost their lives by the capsizing of the Margate surf boat "Friend to all Nations" in attempting to assist a vessel in distress at sea, 2nd Dec. 1897.'

STEPHEN CLAYSON
Coxswain *from* 1905 *to* 1926.

Stephen Clayson joined the lifeboat service in 1883, and became second coxswain in July 1904. He became coxswain of the Margate lifeboat in October 1905 and remained in charge until his retirement in 1926 at the age of seventy. He was afloat on life-saving service on 235 occasions and held the silver medal awarded by the National Lifeboat Institution for the rescue in January 1905 of the crew of the ketch *Malvoisin* in a force nine gale.

The lifeboat *Eliza Harriet* launching from the western slipway on Margate jetty. The slipways were constructed in 1898, one each side of the jetty, for the two lifeboats at that time on station. The *Eliza Harriet* was launched 105 times and saved 152 lives between 1898 and 1927. It was on this boat that Coxswain Clayson carried out the rescue of the crew from the ketch *Malvoisin*, which took over ten hours under sail. It was not until 1925 that Margate received her first engined lifeboat.

Lifeboat *Civil Service No. 1* in the boathouse on the eastern slipway during the naming ceremony of the new motor lifeobat, 12 September 1925. The boat was named *The Lord Southborough* by Lady Southborough, wife of the chairman of the Civil Service Lifeboat Fund.

The Lord Southborough after launching on 12 September 1925. This craft saved 269 lives during her service as Margate lifeboat, and in May 1940 rescued 600 men from the beaches at Dunkirk during the evacuation of the British Expeditionary Force from France. She was replaced in March 1951.

The Lord Southborough outward bound from the eastern slipway on Margate jetty. The buildings in the background include, on the left, the hotels of Fort Crescent, in the centre, the Britannia public house and the tower of Holy Trinity Church, and on the right, Cobbs Brewery.

The steam yacht *Sumurun* ran on to a sandbank off Margate on 19 August 1921 while on a voyage from Southampton to Brightlingsea. Margate lifeboat succeeded in taking off Captain Wringe and his seven crew and landed them at the pier. The crew were looked after by Mr Edward S. Whithead (centre of photograph in white cap), the local representative of the Shipwrecked Mariners' Society. The *Sumurun*, owned by Lord Sackville, was later refloated and taken to Whitstable.

The *London Belle*, a 738-ton paddle steamer built in 1893 by Denny Brothers of Dumbarton. She was one of a fleet of seven paddlers owned by Belle Steamers, connecting Margate and Ramsgate with Clacton, Walton, Felixstowe, Lowestoft and Southend. She was broken up at Grays in Essex in 1929.

The *Southend Belle*, another of the Belle paddlers, weighing 570 tons and built in 1896, again by Denny Brothers. She is seen here in 1905 leaving Margate jetty. The *Southend Belle* survived until 1946 when she was broken up in Holland.

The *Golden Eagle*, owned by the General Steam Navigation Company, was another paddle steamer typical of those that brought many thousands of holiday-makers to Margate each summer. Built in 1909 on Clydebank, she was of 793 tons, and survived until 1951.

The paddle steamer *Royal Sovereign* was built on the Clyde by the Fairfield Shipbuilding and Engineering Company in 1893. She operated a service six days a week from London, Old Swan Pier, to Southend, Margate and Ramsgate, and return. At 891 tons, she was fitted with telescopic funnels that retracted into their casings, and a mast that could be lowered, thus allowing her to reach her London terminal above London Bridge. She made her final voyage to the shipbreakers in Holland in February 1930.

The ketch *Kate* was driven ashore at Newgate Gap during a north-easterly gale on 12 April 1913. Following the removal of her cargo, the ketch was towed off on 17 April and taken to Margate harbour.

The four-masted steamer *Coronel*, registered at Kragero in Norway, ran aground on the Longnose Rock on 10 February 1907. The vessel was on a voyage from Rotterdam to Barry Docks for repairs when she became stranded in dense fog. The Margate lifeboat gave assistance and, with the help of the Ramsgate tug *Aid*, the *Coronel* was refloated the same evening.

The SS *Dunvegan* registered at Boston, Lincolnshire, and of 250 tons, dragged her anchors during a gale in the early hours of 28 April 1919, and nine crew were rescued by the Margate lifeboat under the command of Coxswain Stephen Clayson. Captain Spreight and the mate remained aboard, and the *Dunvegan* was driven ashore opposite Fort Paragon at 4.00 a.m. the same morning.

HM Minesweeper *Taymouth* ashore at Westbrook after dragging her anchor on 20 September 1914. Trenches were dug around the vessel, and she was eventually pulled clear and refloated by a tug on 21 October.

TRANSPORT

Construction of the tramway system operated by the Isle of Thanet Electric Tramways and Lighting Company commenced in 1899, and the route from Westbrook to Ramsgate opened on 6 July 1901. Tram 10, one of the original batch supplied by the St Louis Car Company, USA in 1901, is seen here, having recently been repainted, outside the terminus at Westbrook in the late 1920s.

Margate railway station, *c.* 1875. The London, Chatham & Dover Railway opened a service from
Faversham to Whitstable on 1 August 1860, and the line was extended to Margate, Broadstairs and
Ramsgate Harbour on 5 October 1863.

A similar view of the station, *c.* 1875. A train has arrived from Ramsgate and Broadstairs and waits to
continue its journey to Herne Bay, Whitstable, Faversham and London.

The French aviator, Henri Salmet, flying his Bleriot 80 hp monoplane at Margate during the *Daily Mail* aeroplane tour, 13 August 1913. The plane arrived at Margate by road and flew from a grass strip in what is now Eastern Esplanade. In the background can be seen the Queens Highcliffe Hotel, while in the foreground a police sergeant keeps an eye on the large crowd.

Aeroplanes at Margate, 31 May 1912. Two Short S.27 training biplanes had flown in from Eastchurch on the Isle of Sheppey the previous day together with a Short S.34 Tractor biplane, all three of which are lined up here.

The Graf Zeppelin flies over Sweyn Road during the evening of Saturday 26 April 1930. This view was taken by local photographer Edward Cox of 80 Sweyn Road. The shop front on the left is that of Percy Samson, a builder and decorator at 68 Sweyn Road. The house in the right foreground is 29 Sweyn Road, while in the centre background is the Queen's Highcliffe Hotel. The Graf Zeppelin made its first flight at Friedrichshafen in Germany on 18 September 1928, was 775 feet long and 110 feet high. It carried a crew of 43 and had a top speed of 80 mph. By the time she appeared over Margate in 1930, the craft had already completed a round-the-world trip with twenty passengers on board. The Graf Zeppelin completed 590 flights and more than a million miles before she was scrapped in 1940.

A Margate taxi cab, *c.* 1912, photographed by local photographer W.P. Dobbs.

An old people's outing ready to leave Cecil Square, *c.* 1912. The premises in the background are those of Arthur Thomas, an estate agent and insurance broker, at 1a Cecil Square. The building on the right is at the junction of Cecil Square and Hawley Street.

Mother and son on the promenade at Westbrook, July 1927. The wicker pram suggests that the boy was a patient at the nearby Royal Sea Bathing Hospital, while his mother was staying at a guest house at 39 Canterbury Road. The photograph is by local photographer, Arthur H. Remington of 55 Canterbury Road.

A goat cart and young passenger, *c.* 1910, seen in a photograph by Jetty Studios of Arcade Steps, Margate.

Horse and cart owned by Charles Edward Doughty, a coal merchant, of 16 Cliff Terrace. Mr Doughty had his coal yard at Mill Lane. This photograph, taken in 1910, shows the method of transport employed by those working on the excavations at the Winter Gardens for the removal of the chalk. The excavations are seen on pages 107 and 109.

A Ford delivery van owned by Hancock and Cooper, tobacconists, *c.* 1936, when the van was first registered. It is outside their premises at 7 Grosvenor Place.

Coach and horses outside the Cliftonville Hotel, Ethelbert Crescent, 2 September 1911. Built in 1868 with 300 rooms, the Cliftonville Hotel was one of the largest and most luxurious of the hotels in Victorian and Edwardian Margate. It was demolished in 1962, to be replaced with a bowling alley and Thorley's public house.

Tram 21 turns into Athelstan Road from Ethelbert Terrace and makes its way up towards Northdown Road, *c.* 1930.

Bobby and Sons' first motor van, 1904. Frederick James Bobby came to Margate in 1887 and established a small drapery business at 65 and 67 High Street, at the junction with Queen Street. In 1894 he started a furnishing business at 59 and 61 High Street, and by 1910 had added no. 57 as a ladies' outfitters, and no. 63 became part of the drapers. He now owned the entire block apart from no. 61, which always remained the International Tea Company Stores. The firm became a limited company in 1900 and by 1915 had established branches in Leamington Spa, Folkestone, Eastbourne, Torquay and Bournemouth. A branch also opened at 220–8 Northdown Road, Cliftonville, on 24 April 1913. This was a departmental store with facilities that included a tea lounge with an orchestra and a library, together with a motor-van delivery service throughout Thanet. Frederick Bobby died in 1914, but his business empire survived until 1968 when it was taken over by Debenham's. The Margate store continued until 1970, and the Cliftonville store finally closed on 14 July 1972.

Tram 19 stops for passengers in Marine Terrace in 1932, before continuing its journey to the clock tower. Advertisements appear on the front of the tram for Munro Cobbs furniture store in Northdown Road.

Tram 24 allows a passenger to alight at the clock tower before continuing its journey along Marine Terrace. This tram stops opposite Margate railway station, and reverses on to the eastbound track before returning to Ramsgate.

Northdown Road, Cliftonville, *c.* 1921. Tram 9 passes the furniture store of Messrs Munro Cobb at nos 223 to 229, on its way to Broadstairs. Note that there are no buildings on the far side of the junction with Warwick Road. The building on the right is the Palladium Garage at the junction with Lyndhurst Avenue.

Tram 58, one of the final batch of cars built in 1903 by the British Electric Car Company, leaves the private right of way and enters Northdown Road, *c.* 1922. The southern end of the right of way is shown on page 38, outside Montrose Ladies College in Lower Northdown Road (now Northdown Park Road).

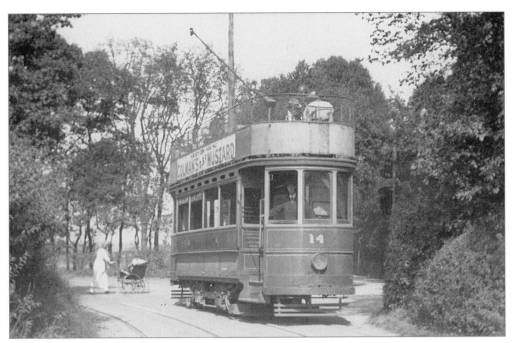

Tram 14 at Northdown, 1924. The tram system closed on 24 March 1937, and services were taken over by buses owned by the East Kent Road Car Company.

The Parade, where buses owned by the East Kent Road Car Company await passengers for Westgate, Birchington, Westwood and Ramsgate. In the foreground is a Daimler Y model, registration number FN 8092, first registered in 1927, on route 1 to Birchington. This was the first double-decked bus operated by the company and continued in service until 1933 when it was scrapped.

A haycart at Northdown, looking across the fields towards Northdown Hill and St Peters. Trams can be seen on Northdown Hill and to the right of them are houses in Mayville Road, St Peters. This postcard was sent on 24 December 1913 to friends in Tenterden by Benjamin Chatterton of Benn Rover, Northdown.

Garlinge level crossing on the London, Chatham & Dover line between Westgate and Margate West railway stations, c. 1926. The houses of Barn Crescent are seen in the background. The crossing closed in 1931 with the building of Bridge Road between Westbrook Avenue and Canterbury Road, but the crossing-keeper's house survived until the late 1980s.

VILLAGES

The Rodney public house, High Street, Garlinge, c. 1938. The public house was built in 1926 on the site of an old barn, and was another house tied to the Cobb Brewery of Margate. At this time the licensee was C.G. Willing. On the left can be seen Wright's delivery van outside their fishmongers shop at 72 High Street.

The Hussar public house on the Canterbury Road, Garlinge, *c.* 1905. This was one of many local houses tied to Thompson & Sons Walmer Brewery. At this time it was advertised as a 'hotel, nursery, fruit and pleasure gardens'. In the early 1920s a road-widening scheme resulted in the demolition of the entire building.

The new Hussar public house was built in 1926. Here the public house is viewed at the junction with High Street, Garlinge in 1933 when the proprietor was Frank Haskins.

Crow Hill, Garlinge, looking towards the High Street, *c*. 1910. The first house on the left was known as Guildford Villa, owned by James Hills, and is now no. 17. Immediately behind this building is the entrance to Ellington Avenue, and now, on the farmland opposite, is the entrance to Coronation Crescent.

By 1920 Crow Hill had been renamed Crow Hill Road. It is seen here viewed from the opposite direction to the photograph above. The first house on the right is now no. 49.

Garlinge Dairy & Poultry Farm, Canterbury Road, Garlinge, *c.* 1912. The farm stood on the south side of Canterbury Road on land now occupied by housing in Noble Gardens. In the background can be seen the tower and spire of St James' Church. The farm was owned at this time by Stanley W. Hedgcock.

Victoria Home for Invalid Children, Canterbury Road, *c.* 1912. At this time the sister in charge was Miss F.E. Court. The buildings are still in use and today form the Westbrook Day Hospital.

Ellington Avenue, Garlinge, looking towards Crow Hill Road, *c.* 1912.

Birds Avenue, Garlinge, *c.* 1912. The first house on the left is no. 48, and in the background can be seen 99 and 101 High Street.

Westfield Road, Garlinge, *c.* 1907. At the time of this photograph the houses seen here were nos 28 to 15, the numbers being consecutive, but following the development of the north side in 1933, they were renumbered with odd numbers, 65 to 39.

Garlinge post office in 1912, when the postmaster was Richard Harlow. The shop was also the local grocery, and remains a post office and grocers to this day. On the left is Crow Hill Road.

Kandy's Tea Shop, Canterbury Road, opposite the Hussar public house, 1933. The owner at this time was Miss Snow. The premises are now 172 Canterbury Road and house a Chinese takeaway. The houses at the back are the new development in Mutrix Road.

Reading Street, *c.* 1910. A group of delivery boys and tradesmen pose for the photographer outside the post office and general stores owned by Walter G. Johnson.

Northdown post office viewed from Friends Corner looking back along what is now Northdown Park Road towards Margate, 1910. The postmaster at this time was Mr G.H. Smart. The building remains and is now known as Honeysuckle Cottage, but the wall that once enclosed Northdown House, on the right of the photograph, has long since disappeared.

Holland House and the coastguard station at Kingsgate, viewed from the Captain Digby public house, c. 1920. Lord Holland's original mansion, Holland House, was built between 1762 and 1768, but following his death in 1774 the estate was left to his son, Charles Fox. The estate was gambled away and the house fell into disrepair, being pulled down in 1808. The buildings seen here were constructed from the materials of the original house.

North Foreland lighthouse, *c.* 1875. The first lighthouse at North Foreland dates from about 1635, but in 1691 a new lighthouse was erected on the same site. The original building and light went through many changes before the building we known today was converted from oil lamps to electricity in 1930.

The cliffs at Kingsgate near the Captain Digby public house, *c.* 1875. The picture shows a 'look-out', one of the follies built by Lord Holland on his estate between 1763 and 1768.

The Captain Digby public house developed from one of the numerous follies built by Lord Holland on his estate between 1763 and 1768. The name of the inn is believed to be taken from Captain Robert Digby, a friend of Lord Holland. This photograph dates from 1875 and was produced by the London Photographic Company.

The Captain Digby public house, 1904. The inn was known in 1809 as 'The Noble Captain Digby', and described as 'a tavern with a good reputation where the landlord exerted every possible civility and attention to accommodate the numerous parties which daily come to dine and drink tea in his house'. The public house has been under the control of various breweries, but is now part of the Thorley Tavern Group.

HOTELS & PUBLIC HOUSES

The Cliftonville Hydro Hotel, Eastern Esplanade, viewed from the entrance to First Avenue, c. 1905.

The Britannia Hotel on Fort Hill with minstrels performing on the lawn outside, *c*. 1870. Before it became a public house, the building was in the grounds of the Cobb Brewery, and was used by the second Francis Cobb as a 'summer house'. Although the public house has long since been rebuilt, the houses on the left in Fort Crescent, dating from the late 1820s, still remain today, little changed from this view.

The Pier Hotel, built in 1834, and the Dukes Head Hotel, *c*. 1870. The two hotels were in Bankside, and faced the entrance to Margate Jetty. In 1878 they were joined together and became the Grand Hotel, which was destroyed in a fire in December 1890. On the site the Hotel Metropole was built, seen on page 20.

The Flamboro boarding house at 32 Athelstan Road, Cliftonville, where a holiday group pose, 1912.

The Six Bells public house stood at the top of the High Street, near to the site of the present building of the same name. Records show that an inn stood on this site in 1722, and during the late eighteenth century it was the venue for local cockfighting under the patronage of the landlord, John Stewart. These buildings were demolished in 1954 as part of the road-building scheme.

The King Edward VII public house at the junction of Dane Valley Road and Millmead Road, 1912. The building was originally a shop premises owned by Charles S. Woodruff, a beer retailer. It became a public house in 1912, tied to Thompson & Sons Walmer Brewery.

The Dane Valley Arms was built in Dane Valley Road in 1929 by the Walmer Brewers, Thompson & Sons Ltd, as the 'Station Hotel'. It was anticipated that a new railway station, Cliftonville Halt, would be built opposite on the line between Margate and Broadstairs, but this did not materialize.

The Wheatsheaf Inn at Northdown dates from 1733. For many years it was owned by Cobb & Co.'s Margate Brewery, as it was in 1935 when this photograph was taken and the landlord was Robert J. Brown.

The Engadine boarding house at 16 Clifton Gardens, 1912. The proprietress was Mrs C. Dobbs and in the background the grocery store owned by William Curtis at 15 Clifton Gardens can be seen.

The Ripley boarding house at 63 Ethelbert Road, Clfitonville, where a group of holiday-makers pose, August 1914. In the background at no. 61 are the shop premises of Penton Brothers, suppliers and hirers of wicker bathchairs, spinal carriages and invalid furniture. Another view of Ethelbert Road can be seen on page 33.

The First & Last public house at the junction of High Street and Ramsgate Road was the first hostelry found by the stage coaches on arrival in town, and the last on departure. It first became licensed in about 1817. On the left of the photograph is Vicarage Place, seen in more detail on page 11.

The Hereward Hotel at 2–26 Gordon Road, Cliftonville, where the residents pose for a holiday snap, *c.* 1920. In the background is the Oval Garage owned by Messrs Carden and Taylor in Percy Road, and behind that are the stables in Cliftonville Mews.

The Ship Hotel at 1 The Parade, *c.* 1905. There is evidence of a 'Ship Inn' on or near this site as early as 1699. This building was the last to be demolished as part of the Fort Road improvement scheme between December 1937 and April 1939, when the present dual carriageway was constructed.

The White Hart Hotel and Lord Nelson public house in The Parade, *c.* 1870. Both buildings were pulled down 1876 to make way for the new White Hart Hotel seen on page 19. On the left is the Albion Hotel at the junct with King Street.

Crooks' boarding house at 9 and 10 Royal Crescent, where the residents pose for a photograph on the sea side of the building, 1920.

The Clieveden boarding house at 6 Union Crescent, where a holiday group pose in the first week of September 1914.

Another group of holiday-makers from the Hereward Hotel in Gordon Road, Cliftonville, July 1912. The stables of the Cliftonville Hotel can be seen in the background.

The Westbrook boarding house at 43 Canterbury Road, Westbrook, where the holiday-makers were photographed on 4 August 1913.

SPORT & LEISURE

A smoking concert held at the Drill Hall, Victoria Road, Margate by No. 10 Company (Margate) Veteran Reserves, 13 January 1912. A programme of music was enjoyed by a large audience in the presence of the commanding officer, Surgeon-Major White, and the mayor, Alderman Edward Coleman.

Margate Football Club, 1936. Back row, left to right: W. Arbuckle (trainer), Millar, Evans, Preedy, Walker, Brophy, Doherty and W. Green (match secretary). Front row, left to right: Robbie, Farr, Lambert, Davie and Clare. They were the winners of the Kent Senior Cup when they defeated Tunbridge Wells 2–1 in the final at Maidstone. They were also the winners of the Kent Senior Shield, the Kent League Cup, and were champions of the Southern League, and have been described as being probably the finest Margate team ever.

Margate Bowling Club champions in 1927. The clubhouse and green was in Northdown Avenue, Cliftonville.

The sixth annual handicap walking match organized by The Lord Byron Friendly Society took place on Whit Monday, 27 May 1912. The start, seen here, was in Park Crescent Road, and the twenty-four starters followed an 11-mile route via Westbrook, Birchington, the Prospect Inn at Minster and Vincent Farm at Garlinge, before returning to Margate. The handicap winner was J. Coulbeck in 1 hour 49 minutes 32 seconds. He had a 20-minute start over the only scratch starter, O.J. Baldwin, who achieved the fastest time of 1 hours 38 minutes 8 seconds, and had won the event in the two previous years. The prizes were presented by Alderman Hughes during a smoking concert at the Lord Byron public house on 30 May.

The Kent County Show, now held each year at Detling, near Maidstone, was held at Margate in July 1926. This postcard was sent by the advertisers in Crewe to a farmer at Sevenoaks on 9 July 1926. The *Isle of Thanet Gazette* tells us that this was the fourth annual show and that it occupied an area of 30 acres on what is now the Palm Bay Estate. The show was opened by the mayor, Councillor Thomas D. Wood.

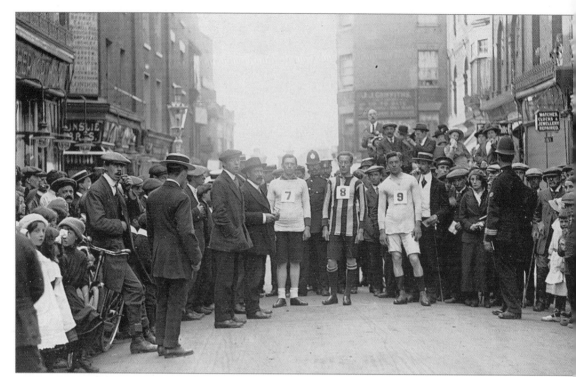

Margate Working Men's Club's first walk, 21 May 1914. The photograph shows the start in the High Street. The shops on the left are, at no. 62, Ainslie Brothers butchers, and at no. 64, Hepworths clothing shop. In the background is John Griffiths drapers at no. 41, at the junction with Bilton Square. The walk started at 5.00 p.m. on a Thursday afternoon, and covered a route of 9 miles, along Grosvenor Place, Tivoli Road, Nash Road, Haine Hospital, and then to St Peters, Reading Street, Northdown, and back into the town centre along Approach Road, Thanet Road and Union Crescent. The press report in the *Thanet Times* the following day informs us that the quickest time was by Hughes in 1 hour 14 minutes 53 seconds, and of the sixteen starters, only one failed to finish.

The Royal Hotel and assembly rooms in Cecil Square, *c.* 1870. Built in 1769, the assembly rooms were a centre where the fashionable society of the day could gather, in particular visitors from London. The building was destroyed by fire in 1882, and was replaced by the building in the photograph below. The buildings on the left stand in Cecil Street, and the one on the extreme left still stands at the junction with Union Crescent. A sign on the building indicates that it was once known as 'Austens Row', and records show it was the site of an eighteenth-century circulating library.

The Hippodrome Theatre stood on the site of the Assembly Rooms, seen in the top photograph. Built as the Grand Theatre in 1897, it reopened as the Hippodrome in September 1905, staging twice nightly music-hall performances. The building was demolished in 1967 and the library and Thanet District Council offices now stand on the site.

The Fort Steps, 1905. In the background is Fort Paragon with the bandstand top right. It is here that the excavations took place for the building of the Winter Gardens as seen on page 107.

Fort Crescent and the Fort bandstand, *c*. 1905. Again in the background is Fort Paragon, seen in more detail on page 30. Note the bathchair waiting for hire in the foreground.

The Pavilion and Winter Gardens. Construction commenced in November 1910 with the removal of the bandstand and over 43,000 cubic yards of chalk. In the background is Fort Crescent with the Fort Lodge Hotel in the centre.

Local workers removing the chalk using nothing more than picks and shovels, before it is taken away by horse and cart. In the background is Fort Crescent, and the tower of Holy Trinity Church, destroyed by enemy action in June 1943.

FORT PAVILION
JULY 13TH 1911

The Pavilion and Winter Gardens were first seen in model form at the end of the 1910 season when the plans were submitted to the Margate Corporation by the Borough Engineer, Mr E. Borg. Within weeks they were approved and the first sod was cut by the mayor, Councillor William Booth Reeve, in November 1910. The chalk was removed in time for the laying of the foundation stone by the mayor on 15 March 1911. The entire pavilion was completed and ready for use by the end of July, and the official opening took place on 3 August. This photograph, dated 13 July 1911, shows a group of workmen putting the finishing touches to one of the approach roads, with Fort Crescent in the background.

Another view of the excavations, shortly before the removal of the bandstand. The gap in the buildings in the background is the entrance to Trinity Square.

The Pavilion and Winter Gardens nearing completion, 12 July 1911. This was just eight months after excavation work began.

The promenade entrance to the Pavilion and Winter Gardens, soon after completion in 1911.

The Pavilion and Winter Gardens viewed from Fort Crescent, 1911.

Croquet lawns at Cliftonville, *c.* 1905. In the background are the High Cliffe Hall and Salisbury House hotels in what was then known as Lewis Avenue. Today these premises are the Wishing Towers Residential Home in Eastern Esplanade.

The Dreamland Amusement Park, 1929. The park was developed on a site purchased by John H. Iles in 1919, the 'scenic railway' being one of the first attractions. Construction began in 1920 and the attraction opened on 3 July 1920. The 'caterpillar' ride was constructed in 1922 and survived until 1979.

The Dreamland Amusement Park, *c.* 1929. The main attractions seen are again the 'caterpillar', together with the 'motor racing cars'. In the background is Belgrave Road.

Aerial view of Dreamland, *c.* 1930. Marine Terrace and the clock tower can clearly be seen in the background, with Belgrave Road on the right. In the foreground is the Southern Railway line connecting Margate with Broadstairs.

PEOPLE & EVENTS

The ruins of a house in Windsor Avenue, Cliftonville, following an air-raid attack on 22 August 1917. This illustration was taken from one of a series of postcards published by Lane, Gentry & Co. of 6 Cecil Square, Margate.

Class one at Salmestone School pose for the camera, 1919.

Margate Grammar School, College Road, 1908. This postcard, dated 22 March 1909 when the headmaster was John Hamilton Douglas, was sent by Wilfred to his 'Grandma' in Twickenham, informing her that 'Mr Douglas wishes us to wear white ties at the annual school concert, will you please send one by the end of the week.'

Salmestone School, College Road, *c.* 1905. The foundation stone for the school was laid in 1895, and the building completed in 1896, the new school being required to accommodate children from what was, at the end of the nineteenth century, a rapidly expanding East Margate.

The Rob Roy Cripples Holiday Home at Gordon House, 9 and 10 Churchfield Place. First recorded in 1816 as 'Mr Turner's day school', by 1876 the building was known as the Victoria Hospital for Children Convalescent Home. In 1894 it was taken over by the YMCA, and in 1903, when this postcard was produced, it was used by The Ragged School Union and Shaftesbury Society. In that year, 382 girls and 20 boys, all cripples from London, attended the home for a summer seaside holiday.

A horse and carriage outside 9 and 10 Churchfield Place, c. 1905. The building still retains the name Gordon House, and is outwardly unaltered to this day.

The fountain, sculptured from Forest of Dean stone, was erected by Councillor A.B. Bourner in memory of his eldest son, 2nd Lieutenant Rowley Moody Nicholson Bourner, and unveiled on 7 November 1922 by the mayor, Councillor Harry B. Smith. Lieutenant Bourner died on 28 March 1918 from wounds received at Passchendaele. The fountain still stands in Lewis Crescent, Cliftonville.

The first postwar visit of ships of the Royal Navy to Margate took place between 29 June and 3 July 1923, when the battleships HMS *Revenge* and *Ramilles*, with a smaller ship, HMS *Princess Margaret*, visited the town. On 30 June, Rear-Admiral W.A.H. Kelly CB, CMG, MVO, and other senior officers (shown on the jetty accompanied by the town sergeant, Mr Swain) came ashore and visited the town hall as guests of the mayor, Councillor William Leach Lewis.

Centenary celebrations of the General Steam Navigation Company, 2 June 1923. Photographed on Margate jetty before boarding the *Golden Eagle* on its first voyage of the season from Margate, as guests of the directors of the GSN Co., are the mayor, Councillor W. Leach Lewis, Aldermen Coleman, Doughty, Hughes and White, and Councillors Smith, Gunnis, Rolfe, Redman, Hoare, Bines, Mayall and Wood. Also present are Mr W. Mercer JP, Mr W. Booth Reeve JP, Colonel E.O. Skey, Mr G.C. Golder (representing Margate Pier & Harbour Co.) and Mr R.C. Bear, the Margate agent for the GSN Co.

Councillor William Leach Lewis and other members of the party on board the *Golden Eagle*. This vessel is also seen on page 62.

Children awaiting the arrival of the mayor and the parade on Mayor's Sunday, 10 November 1912, outside St John's Church. The buildings in the background are 203 and 205 High Street, demolished in 1954 as part of the road-building scheme.

A police constable of the Margate Borough Police outside the Parish Church of St John the Baptist, *c.* 1912.

Margate Borough Police in the parade on Mayor's Sunday, 10 November 1912. The parade follows the annual civic custom of attending the parish church on the Sunday after the election of the new mayor. On this occasion the mayor was Councillor Albert Leon Adutt. This photograph was taken outside the church, close to the Six Bells public house seen on page 92.

Margate Borough Police, 1906. In the centre is the Chief Constable, Mr Alfred Applyard, with his deputy, Inspector Haycock, top centre of the photograph. Chief Constable Appleyard was in charge of the force from 1904 to 1923 when he resigned, handing over to Mr Haycock who was promoted to Chief Constable. The force was formed in 1858 with a complement of six men, one of whom was Daniel Shelvey, the Head Constable. The town had to wait until 1896 before a purpose-built police station was erected adjacent to the existing town hall in the market-place. The building still exists in excellent condition, complete with cells, and now forms part of Margate Museum. This building remained the town police station until the late 1950s when the new police station was built on Fort Hill. On 31 March 1943, the Margate Borough Police Force was amalgamated with the Kent County Constabulary and became 'M' Division of that force.

A group outside Shaftesbury House, a YMCA hostel in Marine Terrace (later Marine Gardens), *c.* 1911. Shaftesbury House is described in more detail on page 24. In the background a horse and carriage can be seen leaving Grosvenor Place.

Crowds gathered outside the Kent Hotel in Marine Terrace for the visit of Princess Alexander of Teck to open the extension to the Margate Cottage Hospital, 22 July 1913. A plaque commemorating this event can still be seen on the outside of the building at the junction of Victoria Road and Thanet Road. This postcard was sent to Gladys Brand at 8 Bishopsgate, London on 29 July by her sister, who is looking out of the top window.

Margate & District postmen photographed in 1906 when the postmaster was Mr J. Rose.

Suffragettes outside the Theatre Royal in Prince's Street, *c.* 1912. In the background can be seen 26 Addington Street, the general stores owned by John and Stephen Peters. On the back of this postcard mention is made of the Pankhurst family, but it is not known if Emmeline Pankhurst or her daughters, Christabel and Sylvia, are present in this group. The author would be grateful for any information about this photograph.

Unveiling of the Margate war memorial, Trinity Square, Sunday 5 November 1922. The unveiling was performed by Lord Harris, and the memorial was later dedicated by the Bishop of Rochester. The town was represented by the mayor, Councillor Harry B. Smith. The memorial cost £2,000, the funds being raised by public subscription, and was executed by Mr Herbert Read of Exeter from a design by Messrs Reeve & Reeve, architects, of 1 Cecil Street, Margate. The memorial is of Cornish granite and consists of an Eleanor cross resting on an octagonal shaft 12 feet high. The shaft stands on an octagonal base on which are inscribed over 400 names of those who fell in the First World War, both military and civilian.

ACKNOWLEDGEMENTS

I am indebted to the following people who have assisted in the research for this book, and have given their time to help complete this project:

John Williams, formerly of Margate Museum, whose enthusiasm and support makes the seemingly impossible very much easier.
Alan Kay for allowing access to his records.
Sid Waldby for sharing his detailed knowledge of the town.

My final thanks again go to my wife, Glenys, who has given much advice and assistance in the selection of photographs for this second volume, and supported me for the duration of this project.

BRITAIN IN OLD PHOTOGRAPHS